PLANT POWER

The Thrify Vegan Cookbook

Delicious faire for budget concsious cooks

BY BRONWEN SKYE

If you're interested in joining my street team to get the next Plant Based cookbooks for FREE, sign up at skyevegan.com/streetteam

TABLE OF CONTENTS

TABLE OF RECIPES

THE THRIFTY VEGAN

Bronwen Skye

Budget Conscious Faire

Healthy Food 365

Cooking on a vegan diet doesn't have to be expensive. There are so many wonderful nutritious staples out there that can satisfy your hunger and your budget. We can start with inexpensive, easy to find vegetables. Then we can toss in some hearty beans and grains - which pack a ton of fiber and nutrition for the punch. Add some spices, a little love or nostalgia (cheesy mac, anyone?) to each recipe and voila!

Pizzas, pastas, curries, nutritious soups, and healthy side dishes make up the better part of this cookbook. Additionally, you'll find a few inexpensive breakfasts and some delicious desserts that won't leave your pocketbook empty, and will satisfy your sweet tooth as well. I've also included a nutritional or thrifty star ingredient for each recipe that you can read about on the bottom of each page. Let's dive in and get started!

ECLECTIC
ENTRÉES

DAN DAN NOODLES

INGREDIENTS

- 16 ounces noodles of choice
- 1 T toasted sesame oil
- ½ cup creamy almond or peanut butter
- 1 t ginger, dried
- 1 t maple syrup
- ¼ cup tamari
- 1 t vinegar
- 1 cup vegetable broth
- 1 T vegetable oil
- 2 red bell peppers, thinly sliced
- 4 scallions, sliced

Prep | 15 min
Cook | 25 min

DIRECTIONS

Cook the noodles according to package directions. Drain, rinse, and return to the pot. Add the sesame oil, tossing to coat.

In a bowl whisk together the almond butter, maple syrup, ginger, tamari, vinegar, and broth until the mixture is smooth. Add water if needed to make a smooth sauce.

Heat the veggie oil in a large skillet over medium high heat. Add bell pepper and sauté for 2 minutes. Add the scallions and sauté for 3 more minutes.

Stir sauce into the skillet with the veggies and cook until heated.

Add the sauce and veggies to the noodles and toss to coat. Heat for 1 minute.

Noodles are inexpensive, you can use any kind. Nut butter is a great source of protein. Red peppers contain antioxidants, vitamins C, B6, and Folate. Scallions, in addition to having antioxidants, are one of the richest sources of vitamin K.

ETHIOPIAN MEAL

INGREDIENTS

RED LENTILS

- 2 small onions
- 2 cloves garlic
- 1 T oil
- 2 T paprika
- 1 t dried ginger
- 1 t turmeric
- 1 t cayenne pepper
- 1 lb. red lentils
- 4 cups vegetable broth

COLLARD GREENS

- 1 T oil
- 1 small red onion, chopped
- 2 jalapenos, chopped
- 2 cloves garlic, crushed
- 1 t salt
- 1 lb. frozen or fresh collard
- greens, chopped

DIRECTIONS

For lentils, purée onion and garlic in a small processor.

Heat oil in a large pot. Add onion purée and spices and cook for 5-10 minutes on medium, careful not to burn the spices.

Add lentils and broth.

Bring to a boil, and lower heat to simmer 20-40 minutes, stirring occasionally. Add water during cooking if necessary.

For collards, warm the oil in a pan. Add onions, peppers, garlic, and salt.

Cook until onions are softened. Add collards, cover and cook until leaves are soft.

Serve with injera, pitas, or tortillas.

Lentils are filling, cheap, and a fantastic source of protein and fiber. Collard greens are an excellent source of vitamin A, vitamin C, calcium, a rich source of vitamin K, and a good source of iron, vitamin B-6, and magnesium. They also contain thiamin, niacin, pantothenic acid, and choline.

PREP TIME

Prep | 25 min
Cook | 45 min

GARLICKY PASTA IN OIL

INGREDIENTS

- 1 lb pasta of choice
- ¼ cup coconut or other oil
- 12 cloves garlic, sliced
- 1 cup parsley, chopped
- 1 t sea salt
- ½ t pepper
- ¼ cup olive oil

Prep | 15 min
Cook | 20 min

DIRECTIONS

Cook pasta according to package directions.

While pasta is cooking, heat oil over medium heat.

Sauté garlic in oil until pale gold.

Remove from heat and add parsley, salt and pepper.

Drain pasta and toss with garlic mixture and olive oil.

Serve hot.

Noodles are inexpensive and when dried last practically forever. Parsley is particularly rich in vitamins A, C, and K. The vitamins and beneficial plant compounds in parsley may improve bone health, protect against chronic diseases, and provide antioxidant benefits.

GREEK PLATE

DIRECTIONS

In a medium saucepan combine 4½ cups water, bulgur wheat, salt, and onion powder. Bring to a boil. Reduce heat and cover, simmer for 10 minutes.

Heat oil in a sauté pan over medium high heat. Add seitan, Italian spices, cumin, and cinnamon. Sauté seitan until lightly browned. Add a little water to deglaze if necessary.

Whisk all tahini sauce ingredients together in a bowl.

Place lettuce on the plate and top with diced pepper and olives.

Serve with bulgur wheat and seitan on the side.

Drizzle with tahini dressing.

Bulgur wheat is a whole grain made from cracked wheat. It's packed with vitamins, minerals and fiber. Fiber-rich foods like bulgur may reduce chronic disease risk, promote weight loss and improve digestion and gut health. Seitan is high in protein and is a good source of minerals like selenium and iron.

INGREDIENTS

- 1½ cups bulgur wheat
- 1 t salt
- ½ t onion powder
- 1 T cooking oil
- 16 oz. seitan, sliced (or other cooked protein)
- 1 t Italian spices
- 2 t cumin
- ½ t cinnamon
- 1 head iceberg or romaine lettuce, chopped
- 1 red bell pepper, diced
- ½ cup black olives, sliced

TAHINI SAUCE
- ¼ cup almond butter
- ¼ cup tahini
- ¼ cup water, or as needed
- ¼ cup lime juice
- 1 t mint flakes
- 1 t salt
- ½ t garlic powder
- ½ t cumin

PREP TIME

Prep | 20 min
Cook | 20 min

INGREDIENTS

- 16 oz. macaroni pasta
- 3 T oil
- 1 T lemon juice
- 1 T nutritional yeast
- 2 t salt
- ½ t pepper
- 1 cup almond milk
- ½ cup water
- 8oz. Daiya cheddar shreds or other shreds
- 2 slices of bread, processed into crumbs
- 2 tomatoes, chopped
- 1 cup frozen peas
- ½ cup parsley, chopped (optional)

Prep | 15 min
Cook | 20 min

MACARONI BAKE

DIRECTIONS

Cook pasta according to package directions. Then drain and then return to the pot.

Heat oven to 350° F.

Melt oil in saucepan on medium low heat. When melted, add lemon juice, nutritional yeast, salt, and pepper. Stir in milk, water, and Daiya shreds. Cook for a few minutes on medium heat, until just blended and a little melty. Stir often to prevent burning. Add paprika and turmeric for color if desired.

Stir cheese sauce into drained macaroni along with tomatoes, peas and parsley.

Transfer pasta to an 8 x 8" pyrex pan or cast iron skillet. Top with breadcrumbs and then spray oil. Bake for 20 minutes uncovered.

Broil for 2-3 minutes or until the top starts to brown.

Garnish with crushed red pepper if desired.

Nutritional yeast is not a must for this recipe, but it has a full spectrum of B vitamins: thiamin, riboflavin, niacin, folate, B6, pantothenic acid, folic acid, niacin. It also includes important minerals like chromium, phosphorus, zinc, selenium, and magnesium.

MEXICAN PIZZA

INGREDIENTS

- 1 can refried beans
- 1 t salt
- 8 flour tortillas (9")
- 8 oz. Daiya shredded pepper jack cheese or any cheese shreds
- 1 pint chunky salsa
- 4 green onions, diced
- 2 jalapenos, thinly sliced

DIRECTIONS

Drain chunky salsa in small strainer, reserve juice.

Add salsa juice to refried beans.

Puncture tortillas with a fork to keep from billowing up, and toast tortillas in a toaster oven or skillet until crispy.

Preheat oven on broiler setting.

Start assembling your pizzas. Starting with one crispy tortilla, add a layer of beans, then place another crispy tortilla on top.

Next, add a couple of tablespoons of drained salsa on top. Sprinkle with shredded cheese. Then add green onions and jalapenos.

Repeat until you've made four pizzas. Lay assembled pizzas on a cookie sheet. Cook the pizzas under the broiler until the cheese melts, about 5 minutes.

Refried beans are inexpensive and low in saturated fat, and very low in cholesterol. It is also a good source of protein, vitamin C, magnesium, phosphorus, potassium, and manganese, and an excellent source of dietary fiber.

PREP TIME

Prep | 15 min
Cook | 10 min

PASTA PUTTANESCA

INGREDIENTS

- 16 oz. spaghetti noodles
- 1 T avocado oil
- 2 cloves garlic, crushed
- 1 pint grape tomatoes, halved
- ½ t mineral salt
- 2 cups vegetable broth
- 1 cup white wine or water
- 15 oz. can of white beans, drained and rinsed
- ½ cup pitted olives
- ½ cup basil, chopped (optional)

Prep | 10 min
Cook | 30 min

DIRECTIONS

Cook noodles according to package directions. Drain and rinse, set aside.

In a medium pot heat oil on medium high heat.

Add garlic and sauté for 1 minute. Add tomatoes, and salt and cook for 2 more minutes.

Add broth and wine and bring to a boil.

Add beans and olives and cook for 5-15 more minutes.

Stir broth mixture into spaghetti in a large pot.

Sprinkle with fresh basil if desired.

Serve with toast if desired.

This pasta is perfect if you can't find spaghetti sauce or are just looking for a change. White beans are packed with folate, vitamin B1 (thiamin), potassium, magnesium, and iron. It's an easy bean to cook with and can be a healthy substitute for the type of starch in potatoes.

PITA PIZZAS

DIRECTIONS

Heat oven to 350°.

Add toppings to pitas and spray lightly with oil if desired.

Bake for 10 minutes.

INGREDIENTS

- 6 pitas
- 1 package (8oz) Daiya cheese shreds or other cheese
- 1 package frozen mushrooms
- 1 jar of roasted red peppers, rinsed and sliced or pint of cherry tomatoes, halved
- Dried or fresh basil
- Any toppings of choice

This is a fast and easy dish that tastes just a little gourmet. Mushrooms contain B vitamins as well as a powerful antioxidant called selenium, which helps to support the immune system and prevent damage to cells and tissues.

PREP TIME

Prep | 5 min
Cook | 10 min

RICH MAN'S MEAL

INGREDIENTS

- Coconut oil
- 1 onion, diced
- 6 cloves garlic, crushed
- 1 lb. bag lentils
- 1 t salt
- ½ t pepper
- Water to cover
- 4 cups cabbage, chopped
- 1 bunch fresh mint, chopped
- ¼ cup lemon juice
- ¼ cup olive oil
- 1 t salt

Prep | 15 min
Cook | 30 min - 2 hrs

DIRECTIONS

Place onion and garlic in large pot with liberal amount of coconut oil. Brown on low heat, the browner the better. This can take 20 minutes to an hour depending on how caramelized you'd like to get the onions.

Once browned to your liking, add lentils, salt, pepper, and enough water to cover plus 2 inches. Bring to a boil, and then turn down heat to medium low. Simmer uncovered for 2 hours or so, stirring occasionally or adding water to prevent sticking. You cannot over-cook. By the same token if you are in a hurry, cook at least 30 minutes on medium with less water. Feel free to add water as needed during cooking.

To make topping, add coleslaw mix, mint, lemon juice, olive oil, and 1 t salt to a large bowl and toss.

Serve lentils in bowl with liberal amount of coleslaw on top. Serve dish alone or with Middle-Eastern bread.

We call this Rich Man's Meal because it's so cheap to make that if you eat it every day, you'll be rich! Lentils stabilize blood sugar and help to reduce cholesterol since it contains high levels of soluble fiber. Cabbage is a powerhouse of nutrition that contains powerful antioxidants, including poly-phenols and sulfur compounds.

SESAME NOODLES

DIRECTIONS

Cook noodles al dente according to package directions. Drain and rinse.

Whisk together peanut butter, soy sauce, olive oil, maple syrup, tahini, sesame oil, and cayenne. Add to cooked noodles and toss to coat.

Toss in cabbage, carrots, scallions and sesame seeds.

Garnish with cilantro if desired.

INGREDIENTS

- 8 oz. udon noodles
- ⅓ cup peanut butter
- ⅓ cup soy sauce or tamari
- ¼ cup olive oil
- 2 T maple syrup
- 2 T tahini
- 2 T toasted sesame oil
- ¾ t cayenne pepper
- ½ cabbage, shredded
- 2 carrots, shredded
- 4 scallions, sliced
- 2 T toasted sesame seeds
- Cilantro for garnish (optional)

Noodles are featured for their hardiness in storage and ease on your pocketbook. Peanut butter is great for flavor and protein. Cabbage is included for its star nutritional value and inexpensiveness. Carrots are a particularly good source of beta carotene, fiber, vitamin K1, potassium, and antioxidants.

PREP TIME
Prep | 20 min
Cook | 15 min

SPICY MONGOLIAN CHICK'N

INGREDIENTS

- 1 package (10 oz.) Gardein chick'n strips

  (or other protein - tofu, beans, etc.)

- Cooking oil

- 1 onion, finely chopped

- 1 t garlic, dried

- 1 t ground ginger

- 1-2 t crushed red pepper

- 1 bunch broccoli florets (fresh or frozen)

- 1 red bell pepper, seeded and sliced

- 3 T Soy Sauce

- 1 T water

- 4 scallions, sliced

- 1 T toasted sesame oil

- Rice, 2 cups

Prep | 20 min
Cook | 30 min

DIRECTIONS

Prepare rice.

Sauté Chick'n in oil until browned, then set aside and keep warm.

Heat 1 T oil in large skillet. On medium high heat add onion, garlic, ginger, and red pepper flakes. Cook for 3 minutes or until onions start to soften.

Add broccoli, bell pepper, soy sauce and water. Cover and steam for 4 minutes, or until broccoli is just cooked.

Remove from heat. Stir in chick'n, scallions and sesame oil.

Serve over rice.

Broccoli is a great source of vitamins K and C, a good source of folate and also provides potassium, fiber, and vitamin C. It builds collagen, which forms body tissue and bone, and helps cuts and wounds heal

SUMMER HARVEST PIZZA

DIRECTIONS

In a large skillet, heat oil over medium-high heat and sauté onions with salt and pepper until soft and lightly caramelized, about 20 to 30 minutes.

Preheat oven to 450° F.

Spread a layer of hummus evenly over the pizza crust. Use ½ of everything so you can do both pizzas.

On top of the hummus, arrange the spinach, caramelized onions, apple slices, and squash. Spray the pizza and crust with oil.

Bake for 10-12 minutes until the crust is lightly browned or golden. Then broil for 2 minutes.

Season with salt and pepper. Slice and enjoy!

INGREDIENTS

- 1 T coconut or other oil
- 1 onion, thinly sliced
- 1 t salt
- ½ t black pepper
- 2 tubs of hummus (7 oz each.)
- 2 Pre-made pizza crusts
- 1 package frozen squash cubes, thawed
- 1-2 cups baby spinach or arugula (fresh or frozen)
- 1 gala apple, thinly sliced
- Spray oil

Squash is high in vitamins A, B6, and C, folate, magnesium, fiber, riboflavin, phosphorus, and potassium. As a serious nutritionally power-packed veggie, yellow squash is also rich in manganese. This mineral helps to boost bone strength.

PREP TIME

Prep | 15 min
Cook | 15 min

SWEET POTATO HASH WITH CHILI OIL

INGREDIENTS

- 2 large sweet potatoes, grated
- 1 package frozen kale
- 1 red bell pepper, thinly sliced
- 1 onion, half-moon sliced
- 2 t salt
- ¼ cup cooking oil, non-coconut

- CHILI OIL
- ¼ cup refined coconut oil
- 2 T crushed red pepper
- ½ t cumin
- ½ t paprika
- ¼ cup olive oil

- Rice
- Cilantro, chopped, for garnish (optional)

Prep | 20 min
Cook | 25 min

DIRECTIONS

Preheat oven to 375° F.

Toss potatoes, kale, bell peppers, and onions with salt and cooking oil and place in a 9 x 11" baking pan. Bake at 375 for 20 minutes. Then broil for 5 minutes.

Meanwhile, make the CHILI OIL: Place coconut oil and crushed pepper in small non-stick skillet. Cook on low heat until peppers stop sizzling (about 10 minutes). Remove from heat and add cumin and paprika. When mixture cools down, add olive oil.

Serve hash over rice, and drizzle with chili oil. Garnish with cilantro.

Extracts of orange sweet potatoes and sweet potato peels have also been found to have anti-cancer properties in test-tube studies. Orange-fleshed sweet potatoes are one of the richest natural sources of beta-carotene, a plant-based compound that is converted to vitamin A in your body.

YUMMY EASY CHILI

DIRECTIONS

If using tempeh, mash the tempeh with a potato masher until it is ground up.

Put all the ingredients together in large pot. Bring to a boil, stirring occasionally.

Add water if necessary.

Lower heat to medium and simmer until the nuts are tender, for about 30 minutes.

INGREDIENTS

- 2 bricks tempeh (or 16 oz. of any beans)
- 3 large tomatoes, chopped
- 1 large onion, chopped
- 2 cloves garlic, crushed
- 2 jalapenos, chopped
- 1 large green chili, chopped
- ½ cup peanuts or cashews
- ¼ cup apple cider vinegar (optional)
- 2 T chili powder
- 2 t cumin
- 1½ t salt
- 1 t oregano
- 1 t tabasco sauce
- ½ t cocoa powder

Tempeh, a good source of calcium, it may decrease cholesterol levels, oxidative stress and appetite while improving bone health. Tempeh contains prebiotics, which improve digestive health and reduce inflammation. It's also an excellent source of antioxidants and micro-nutrients such as manganese, phosphorus, magnesium, and riboflavin. In this recipe, you'll never even know it's there.

PREP TIME

Prep | 20 min
Cook | 30 min

CAPTIVATING
CURRIES

ALOO GOBI

INGREDIENTS

- 2 T coconut oil or cooking oil
- 1 large onion, sliced
- 3 cloves garlic, crushed

  SPICES
- 1 T curry powder
- 1 t cumin
- 1 t ginger
- 1 t salt
- 1 t turmeric

- 2 large potatoes, cut into bite-sized pieces
- 2 cups vegetable broth
- 1 can (14 oz) coconut milk
- 1 head cauliflower, cut into florets
- 2 large tomatoes, diced (or 1 can diced)
- 1 cup frozen peas
- ¼ cup cilantro, chopped
- 2 cups rice

Prep | 20 min
Cook | 30 min

DIRECTIONS

Prepare rice.

Sauté onion and garlic in oil for about 3 minutes in a large pot.

Add the spices and cook for 3 more minutes. Deglaze the pan with ½ cup water.

Add potatoes, vegetable broth, and coconut milk and bring to a boil. Reduce heat to simmer for 10 minutes.

Add cauliflower and tomatoes and bring back to a low boil. Simmer for 10 more minutes.

Add peas and stir.

Remove from heat, and then stir in cilantro.

Serve over rice.

This is a large dish, it serves 4 or more. Cauliflower is a cruciferous vegetable that is naturally high in fiber and B-vitamins. It provides antioxidants and phytonutrients that can protect against cancer.

ASSAM RASSAM

INGREDIENTS

- 2 cups rice
- 2 cans (14 oz.) coconut milk
- 3 red bell peppers, chopped
- 2 t coriander powder
- 2 t cumin
- 2 t salt
- 1 t fenugreek powder (optional)
- 1 t turmeric
- ½ cup cilantro, chopped

DIRECTIONS

Prepare rice.

Add all remaining ingredients to a large pot and bring to a boil.

Lower heat and simmer for 15 minutes or until peppers are soft.

Serve over cooked rice.

Garnish with additional cilantro if desired.

TThe medium-chain fatty acids in coconut milk and coconut oil are highly prized for their health benefits. It also contains lauric acid, a medium chain saturated fatty acid that exhibits antimicrobial and anticancer properties.

PREP TIME

Prep | 10 min
Cook | 25 min

APPLE AND ONION CURRY

INGREDIENTS

- Coconut oil or other oil
- 3 medium onions, or 4 small ones, sliced
- 5 cloves garlic, crushed
- 1 T curry powder
- 1 t cayenne pepper
- 1 t salt
- ½ t black pepper
- ½ t coriander
- ½ t cumin
- 1 large apple, or 2 small, chopped
- 1 package tofu, cubed (or other cooked protein)
- ½ cup raisins
- ¾ cup nuts, roughly chopped
- 1 cup veggie broth
- 1 can (14 oz) coconut milk
- Cilantro, chopped for garnish
- 2 cups rice

Prep | 20 min
Cook | 30 min

DIRECTIONS

Prepare rice.

In large sauté pan on medium, heat liberal amount of oil. Add onions, garlic, and spices. Sauté until onions are soft.

Add apple, tofu, raisins, nuts, veggie broth, and coconut milk.

Bring to a boil on high, then lower heat to medium low and simmer for 20 minutes.

Serve over rice and garnish with cilantro.

Onions contain antioxidants and compounds that fight inflammation, decrease tri-glycerides and reduce cholesterol levels. All of these things may lower heart disease risk. Their potent anti-inflammatory properties may help reduce high blood pressure and protect against blood clots.

BHINDI MASALA

DIRECTIONS

Prepare rice.

Grind onions and garlic into a paste in a mini food processor.

Heat oil in a pan on medium heat.

Add onion mixture and spices and sauté for 5 minutes.

Add okra, jalapeno, and bell pepper. Cook, covered, for 15 minutes on medium.

Add tomatoes. Cook, covered 5 more minutes

Stir in lemon juice and cilantro.

Serve over rice.

INGREDIENTS

- Cooking oil
- 2 medium onions, coarsely chopped
- 4 cloves garlic
- 2 t salt
- 1 t coriander
- 1 t cumin
- 1 t ginger
- 1 t turmeric
- 1 lb. fresh or frozen okra, sliced
- 2 jalapenos, chopped
- 1 large bell pepper, chopped
- 2 large tomatoes, diced (or 1 can diced)
- 1 cup cilantro, chopped
- 2 T lemon juice
- 2 cups rice

Okra is rich in magnesium, folate, fiber, antioxidants, and vitamins C, K1, and A. It may lower cholesterol, and some studies show that it may even have anticancer properties.

PREP TIME

Prep | 20 min
Cook | 25 min

CAULIFLOWER QUINOA CURRY

INGREDIENTS

- 1 cup quinoa
- 1 cup frozen peas
- 2 T oil
- ½ t fennel seeds
- ½ t cumin
- ½ t turmeric
- 4 t curry powder
- 1 cup veggie broth
- 1 medium head cauliflower, cut into florets
- ⅓ cup almond milk
- ¾ cup whole roasted cashews
- ¼ cup cilantro, chopped

Prep | 15 min
Cook | 30 min

DIRECTIONS

Bring pot of water to boil. Add quinoa, and cook, uncovered, 11 to 14 minutes, until grain is tender but still slightly crunchy. Place peas in strainer. Drain quinoa over peas, set aside.

Heat oil in large pot over medium high heat. Add fennel, curry powder, cumin, and turmeric and toast for 30 seconds. Stir in broth and bring to a boil.

Add cauliflower and cashews, and return to boil. Reduce heat to medium, cover and simmer 4 minutes until florets are tender, stirring occasionally. Remove from heat.

Add the rest of the ingredients. Serve a la carte or with mango chutney.

Quinoa is gluten-free, high in protein and one of the few plant foods that contain sufficient amounts of all nine essential amino acids. It is also high in fiber, magnesium, B vitamins, iron, potassium, calcium, phosphorus, vitamin E, and a host of beneficial antioxidants.

GREENS CURRY

INGREDIENTS

- 15 oz. cooked chickpeas, drained and rinsed
- 1 can coconut milk
- 1-2 T curry powder
- 1 T lime juice
- 1-2 t salt
- ⅛ t cinnamon
- 1 bunch chard or kale, fresh or frozen, finely chopped
- 1 bunch broccoli, fresh or frozen, cut florets
- 2 cups rice

DIRECTIONS

Prepare rice as desired.

In a large pot add, chickpeas, coconut milk, curry powder, lime juice, salt, and cinnamon.

Bring to a low boil over medium-high heat.

Stir in chard and return to a boil.

Reduce heat, cover, and simmer for 5 minutes.

Add broccoli and simmer for 5 more minutes.

Serve over rice.

Chickpeas contain protein, folate, fiber (both insoluble and soluble), iron, and phosphorus. They also contain fatty acids including linoleic and oleic acids. The benefits of chickpeas include the ability to improve digestion, prevent heart diseases, and stabilize blood pressure levels. They also boost bone, skin, and hair health..

PREP TIME

Prep | 20 min
Cook | 25 min

KITCHARI

INGREDIENTS

- 2 T refined coconut oil
- 1 small onion, chopped
- 1 t mineral salt, or to taste
- 1 T curry powder
- 1 t turmeric
- 6 cups water
- 1 cup rice, rinsed
- 1 cup lentils, rinsed

- Root vegetable, chopped (optional)
- Green vegetable, chopped (optional)
- Cilantro for garnish (optional)

Prep | 10 min
Cook | 35 min

DIRECTIONS

In a large pot, heat oil in pan over medium.

Add onion and salt. Cook until light brown. Stir in curry powder and turmeric.

Add water, rice, and lentils, and bring to a boil.

Bring heat to medium low and cook for 20 minutes, adding water as necessary.

Stir in the root vegetable if using. Cook for 10 more minutes.

If using a green vegetable, stir into pot. Cook for 10 more minutes.

Garnish with Cilantro.

Kitchari is a traditional Indian meal that is nourishing and easy to digest. Therefore it is often used for cleansing, detoxing, and healing. With turmeric added it has anti-inflammatory properties. Rice can serve as a good source of B vitamins (thiamin, niacin, and riboflavin) and iron. Rice is also an excellent source of manganese and magnesium.

YELLOW THAI CURRY WITH SPINACH

DIRECTIONS

Prepare rice.

In a large pot, heat oil over medium high heat.

Add onion, pepper, garlic, ginger, curry powder, salt, and cinnamon, and sauté for 5 minutes, stirring frequently. Deglaze with a little water if necessary.

Add chickpeas, coconut milk, and lime juice and bring to a simmer.

Add tomatoes and peas and cook for 5 minutes.

Add spinach and cook until heated, 2-5 minutes.

Serve curry over rice.

INGREDIENTS

- 1 T coconut oil
- 1 small onion, diced
- 1 green pepper, chopped
- 2 t garlic, dried
- 1 t ginger, dried
- 2 t curry powder
- 1 t salt
- ½ t cinnamon
- 15 oz. cooked chickpeas, drained and rinsed
- 1 can coconut milk
- 2 T lime juice
- 1 tomato, diced (or ½ can diced)
- 10. oz. frozen peas
- 5 oz. baby spinach, fresh or frozen
- 2 cups rice

Spinach is an excellent source of vitamin K, vitamin A, vitamin C, and folate as well as being a good source of manganese, magnesium, iron, and vitamin B2. Vitamin K is important for maintaining bone health and it is difficult to find vegetables richer in vitamin K than spinach.

PREP TIME

Prep | 15 min
Cook | 25 min

SOUPS AND STEWS

BROCCOLI CHEDDAR SOUP

INGREDIENTS

- 2 T oil
- 1 medium onion, finely chopped
- 3 cloves garlic, crushed
- 4 cups veggie broth
- 3 small potatoes, ½ inch diced
- 2 t nutritional yeast
- ½ t pepper
- 1 bunch broccoli florets, broken into bite sized pieces
- 8 oz. Daiya cheddar cheese shreds or other
- 1 T light miso, mixed with a little water (optional)

Prep | 20 min
Cook | 25 min

DIRECTIONS

IIn large pot over medium heat add oil, onion and garlic and sauté until slightly browned.

Add veggie broth, potatoes, nutritional yeast, and pepper, and bring to a low boil. Lower heat to simmer and cook partially covered for 15 minutes.

Stir in broccoli and Daiya cheese and cook on medium heat until cheese is melted, about 5 minutes.

Remove from heat, stir in miso and serve.

Potatoes are stuffed with phytonutrients, which are organic components of plants that are thought to promote health, according to the USDA. Phytonutrients in potatoes include carotenoids, flavonoids, and caffeic acid..

CELERY CHOWDER

DIRECTIONS

Add chopped celery and onion, veggie broth, and thyme to a large pot.

Bring to a boil and then simmer until tender (about 20 minutes).

Immersion blend or put soup in blender and purée.

Return to pot. Stir in veggies and bring back to a boil. Simmer for a few minutes.

Stir in non-dairy milk, remove from heat, and serve.

INGREDIENTS

- 1 bunch celery, chopped
- 1 onion, chopped
- 6 cups veggie broth
- ½ t thyme
- 6-8 cups any chopped veggies, peas corn, etc.
- 1 cup non-dairy milk

Celery is rich in antioxidants and other bioactive compound. It's vitamin A supports immunity skin, and eye health, and has been linked to retaining lung strength as well as slowing age-related cognitive decline. Celery's vitamin K helps blood to clot and protects bone density.

PREP TIME

Prep | 15 min
Cook | 30 min

INGREDIENTS

- 1 T oil

- 1 large onion, chopped

- 2 t salt

- 2 T curry powder (or to taste)

- 4 cups water

- 2 cans chickpeas or garbanzos

- 1 can (14 oz) coconut milk

- 1 T lemon or lime juice

- 1 10 oz. bag baby spinach (fresh or frozen)

- 3 T chopped cilantro

- 2 cups rice, cooked

Prep | 15 min
Cook | 25 min

CHICKPEA COCONUT SOUP

DIRECTIONS

Heat oil in large pot over medium heat.

Add the onion and salt and sauté, stirring frequently, until the it starts to color and soften, about 10 minutes.

Add the curry powder, stir for a few seconds, and then deglaze with 4 cups of water.

Add the chickpeas. Bring to low boil. Simmer for 10 minutes.

Purée the soup in a blender or immersion blender.

Return the soup to the stove and stir in the coconut milk and lime juice.

If using frozen spinach, stir it in at this time and bring soup back to a low boil. If using fresh spinach stir in and cook for only 2 more minutes.

For serving, ladle soup into bowls and add a scoop of rice.

Turmeric is the spice that gives curry powder its yellow color and is praised around the world for its medicinal qualities. The curcumin found in turmeric has both anti-inflammatory and antioxidant properties. Curcumin also protects against heart disease and may prevent certain cancers.

CHICKPEA NOODLE STEW

INGREDIENTS

- 2 T oil
- 1 onion, thinly sliced
- 2 cloves garlic, crushed
- ½ t celery seeds
- ½ t thyme
- ½ t rosemary
- ½ t pepper
- 8 oz. fresh or frozen sliced cremini mushrooms
- 2 T cooking wine (or water)
- 2 cups vegetable broth
- 6 cups water
- 3 carrots, thickly sliced
- 2 cans chickpeas or garbanzos
- 8 oz. udon or other noodles
- 1 handful of greens (fresh or frozen), chopped
- ⅓ cup light miso paste (optional)
- Salt to taste

PREP TIME

Prep | 20 min
Cook | 30 min

DIRECTIONS

Over medium high heat sauté onion and garlic in oil in a large pot for 10 minutes. Add spices and sauté for 5 more minutes.

Deglaze the pot with cooking wine or water. Add broth, water, carrots, chickpeas, and frozen mushrooms. Bring to a boil.

Once boiling, break the noodles in half and throw them in. Cook for 5 minutes.

Add greens and cook for 5 more minutes.

If using: mix miso paste with ⅓ cup of water to emulsify.

Remove soup from heat, and add miso or salt.

Miso is rich in essential minerals and a good source of various B vitamins, vitamins E, K and folic acid. As a fermented food, miso provides the gut with beneficial bacteria; good gut health is known to be linked to our overall mental and physical wellness.

ITALIAN WEDDING SOUP

INGREDIENTS

- 2 T oil
- ½ cup onion, chopped
- 2 cloves garlic, crushed
- 4 ribs celery, sliced
- 2 carrots, chopped
- 6 cups veggie broth
- 5 cups water
- 1 tomato, chopped (or ½ can diced)
- 16 oz. small pasta
- 16 oz. seitan, chopped (or other cooked protein)
- ½ cup nutritional yeast
- 6 cups baby greens
- 1 cup basil, fresh chopped (optional)

DIRECTIONS

Heat oil in a large pot over medium high heat.

Add onion and garlic and sauté for 3 minutes. Add celery and carrot, and sauté for 5 more minutes.

Add veggie broth, water and tomato and bring to a boil.

Add pasta. Reduce heat and cook for time recommended by pasta package directions. Stir frequently. Add water if necessary.

Once pasta is al dente, stir in the seitan (or other protein) and nutritional yeast.

Add baby greens and basil (if using) and stir until wilted, about 2 minutes.

This soup is easy, delicious, and satisfying. Baby greens provide a healthy dose of vitamin A, vitamin C, vitamin K and folate and potassium. Mixed greens may also contribute some calcium and iron. Blends of greens with more spinach may provide slightly more protein.

PREP TIME

Prep | 20 min
Cook | 30 min

MUSHROOM AND BARLEY SOUP

INGREDIENTS

- 1 T oil
- 2 cups mushrooms, sliced (fresh or frozen)
- ½ t salt
- ½ t pepper
- 1 onion, finely chopped
- 3 stalks celery, thinly sliced
- 2 carrots, sliced
- ½ cup parsley (or any green), chopped
- 6 cups of veggie broth
- 2 cups water
- 1 cup quick cooking pearled barley
- ½ cup of almond milk (or other)

Prep | 20 min
Cook | 35 min

DIRECTIONS

Heat oil in a large pot over medium high heat. Add mushrooms, salt, and pepper and sauté for 7 minutes.

Add onion, and cook for 7 more minutes.

Add celery, carrot, and parsley, and cook for 5 more minutes.

Add broth and water and barley, and bring to a boil. reduce heat to a simmer.

Cover and cook for about 10 minutes, or follow barley package cooking directions.

Stir in milk.

Add water if necessary.

Barley's claim to nutritional fame is based on its being a very good source of molybdenum, which activates enzymes that help break down harmful sulfites and prevent toxins from building up in the body. Manganese, dietary fiber, and selenium, and a good source of copper, vitamin B1, chromium, phosphorus, magnesium, and niacin round out this grain.

SAVORY SQUASH AND APPLE SOUP

DIRECTIONS

Heat oil in large pot over medium-high heat. Add onion, and cook until lightly browned, about 15 min. Add ginger and garlic and cook for 2 minutes. Deglaze with water if necessary. Add squash, apples, turmeric, salt, garam masala, and pepper and stir until fragrant, about 2 minutes.

Add stock and bring to a boil. Lower heat to simmer and then cover. Cook, stirring occasionally, until squash and apple are tender, about 15 minutes. Using an immersion blender or food processor, puree the soup, then return to saucepan. Stir in the lime juice and keep warm.

In a small pan and add coconut oil, cumin, mint, paprika and a shake of salt and pepper. Cook over medium-low heat stirring.

Pour soup into bowls, and top with a drizzle of the spiced oil.

INGREDIENTS

- 2 T oil
- 1 large onion, finely chopped
- 1 t dried ginger
- 2 t dried garlic
- 36 oz. frozen cubed squash (or fresh)
- 2 Granny Smith apples, peeled and cubed
- 1 t turmeric
- 1 t salt
- ½ t garam masala
- ½ t pepper
- 4 cups veggie broth
- 1 t lime juice
- ¼ cup refined coconut oil or other
- ½ t cumin
- ½ t dried mint
- ½ t paprika

Granny Smith apples promote the growth of good bacteria in the colon because of their high content of non-digestible compounds, like dietary fiber and polyphenols. When you eat a Granny Smith the compounds reach the colon, where they ferment and grow friendly bacteria colonies there.

PREP TIME

Prep | 15 min
Cook | 30 min

SWEET POTATO CORN CHOWDER

INGREDIENTS

- 1 T vegetable oil
- 2 green peppers, sliced
- 2 red bell peppers, diced
- 1 carrot, shredded
- 1 onion, diced
- 1 teaspoon salt
- 10 oz. frozen corn
- 3 cups vegetable broth
- 2 sweet potatoes, chopped
- 1 bay leaf
- 2 T lime juice
- Parsley, chopped (optional)

Prep | 20 min
Cook | 40 min

DIRECTIONS

Heat oil over medium high heat in a large pot. Sauté green pepper, red pepper, carrot, onion, and salt until onion is translucent, about 10 minutes.

Add corn, broth, and sweet potatoes. Bring to a boil, and then the lower heat and cover. Simmer for 20 minutes, or until the sweet potatoes are tender.

Purée half of the chowder. Use an immersion blender, or transfer half of the chowder to a blender, purée until smooth and then add back to the soup.

Stir in lime juice, add water if necessary. Simmer for 5 more minutes.

Garnish with parsley if desired.

Corn contains valuable B vitamins, which are important to your overall health. Corn also provides our bodies with essential minerals such as zinc, magnesium, copper, iron, and manganese. Corn is a good source of the antioxidants caro-tenoids, lutein, and zeaxanthin, which promote eye health.

VEGETABLE BARLEY STEW

DIRECTIONS

In large pot, heat oil on medium.

Stir in onion, garlic, salt and pepper, and sauté for 5 minutes.

Add water, broth, and mushrooms, and heat to boiling.

Add barley and green beans and heat to boiling, and then simmer for 5 minutes.

Add carrots, dark greens, and zucchini and heat to boiling, and then simmer for 5 minutes.

Add tomatoes, and simmer for 5 more minutes.

Garnish with olive oil and nutritional yeast.

Zucchini is rich in antioxidants and anti-inflammatory compounds, including vitamins A and C, glutathione peroxidase, and superoxide dismutase. Eating zucchini regularly reduces oxidation and inflammation within the body. This boosts your immunity and protects against diseases associated with inflammation.

INGREDIENTS

- 1 T oil
- 1 medium onion, cut into chunks
- 2 cloves garlic, crushed (2 t dried)
- 1 t salt
- ½ t pepper
- 5 cups water
- 3 cups veggie broth
- 8 oz. frozen mushrooms
- 1 cup quick cooking pearled barley
- 8 oz. cut green beans
- 1-2 cups shredded carrots
- 2 cups dark greens, chopped (fresh or frozen)
- 2 zucchinis, sliced (optional)
- 2 tomatoes, diced (or 1 can diced)
- Olive oil
- Nutritional yeast

PREP TIME

Prep | 20 min
Cook | 30 min

VEGGIE PHO

INGREDIENTS

- 1 package udon noodles (8 oz.)
- 5 cups vegetable broth
- 1 package frozen mushrooms
- 10 oz. tempeh or tofu or cooked protein
- 1 package bean sprouts
- 1 cup baby greens
- 1 tomato, chopped
- 4 scallions, sliced
- ½ cup fresh basil, chopped (optional)
- 2 T cilantro, chopped (optional)

Prep | 10 min
Cook | 20 min

DIRECTIONS

Cook noodles according to package directions. Set aside.

Cube tempeh or tofu.

Add broth to large pot and add mushrooms. Bring to a boil.

Stir in cooked noodles with the rest of ingredients.

Heat for a couple of minutes.

Serve hot.

Mung bean sprouts offer the iron people need to maintain a healthy body. Iron helps our cells stay strong and devoid of infection. Studies have been conducted showing the importance of iron due to its ability to help kill off damaging pathogens.

WEST AFRICAN PEANUT SOUP

DIRECTIONS

Sauté onion in oil until translucent.

Stir in cayenne, ginger, and carrots and sauté for 2 more minutes. Add potatoes, tomatoes, veggie broth, peanut butter, and maple syrup. Bring soup to a boil. Simmer for 20 minutes.

With a slotted spoon, add soup solids to blender. Working in batches if necessary, purée soup solids. Add cooking liquid if needed. Return soup to the pot. Add the chopped roasted peppers.

Simmer for 10 minutes. Remove from heat. Add sliced scallions.

Serve with warm bread, or over rice.

In addition to being an American favorite, peanut butter has potassium as well as protein which lower the risk of high blood pressure, stroke and heart disease. Peanut butter also contains fiber for your bowel health, healthy fats, magnesium to fortify your bones and muscles, vitamin E, and antioxidants.

INGREDIENTS

- 1 T coconut oil or other oil
- 2 onions, chopped
- 1 t cayenne pepper
- ½ t ground ginger
- 2 carrots, chopped
- 2 small potatoes, chopped
- 2 large tomatoes, roughly chopped (or 1 can diced)
- 4 cups vegetable broth
- 1 cup creamy peanut butter
- 1 t maple syrup
- 1 jar (12 oz.) roasted red peppers, chopped
- 4 scallions, sliced (optional)

PREP TIME

Prep | 25 min
Cook | 45 min

COOL COMPLIMENTS

AVOCADO TOMATO MELT

INGREDIENTS

- 4 English muffins, split
- 2 ripe avocados
- 1 t salt
- 1 t lemon juice
- 2 large tomatoes, chopped (or 1 can diced)
- 1/2 cup chopped fresh basil leaves
- mozzarella vegan shreds, or other shreds
- Nutritional yeast
- Fresh ground pepper

Prep | 10 min
Cook | 15 min

DIRECTIONS

Toast English muffin halves until golden brown. Remove from oven.

Mash avocados with salt and lemon juice.

Top each muffin half with mashed avocados and chopped tomatoes.

Sprinkle chopped basil leaves over the tomatoes. Add a layer of vegan mozz-arella cheese over the basil, sprinkle with nutritional yeast, and black pepper.

Broil prepared muffin halves on a baking sheet for approximately 5 minutes, or until cheese has melted.

Remove from oven and enjoy!

Avocados are a great source of vitamins C, E, K, and B-6, as well as riboflavin, niacin, folate, pantothenic acid, mag-nesium, and potassium. They also provide lutein, beta-carotene, and omega-3 fatty acids.

BROCCOLI CHERRY SALAD

DIRECTIONS

Mix all ingredients together and serve!

INGREDIENTS

- 1 large bunch of broccoli, broken into bite size bits
- ¾ cup dried cherries
- 1 cup vegan mayo
- ¾ cup cashews or almonds
- ½ red onion, diced

Besides being-packed with anti-oxidants, fiber, calcium, and vitamin C, cherries contain a hormone called melatonin which facilitates peaceful sleep. Melatonin is a hormone produced by the pineal gland in the brain. It is known to regulate your sleep and wake cycles and control the internal body clock.

PREP TIME

Prep | 10 min
Cook | 5 min

CELESTIAL CORNBREAD

INGREDIENTS

- Spray oil
- 2 cups corn flour
- 2 t xanthan gum
- 1 t baking soda
- 1 t salt
- 1 cup maple syrup
- 1¼ cups non-dairy milk
- ¼ cup oil, non-coconut

Prep | 10 min
Cook | 25 min

DIRECTIONS

Preheat oven to 400° F.

Spray oil a 9 x 9" baking dish or 12 cup muffin tin.

Mix together dry ingredients, and then wet ingredients separately, then mix both together.

Pour batter into pan and bake for 25 to 30 minutes.

In addition to a host of minerals, maple syrup has 24 antioxidants that help to protect you from many health conditions. Antioxidants are important for the body as they neutralize free radicals, which may cause various diseases. Studies also show that the darker versions of maple syrup are higher in antioxidant content in comparison to lighter ones.

GINGER ROASTED ROOT VEGETABLES

DIRECTIONS

Preheat oven to 425° F.

Roughly chop all veggies.

Toss all ingredients in a large bowl.

Add to lightly oiled baking dish.

Place in oven and bake for 20 minutes.

Remove from oven and stir with spatula, and then bake for 20 more minutes until soft and lightly browned.

Serve warm.

INGREDIENTS

- 2 small beets
- 1 large sweet potato
- 4 carrots
- 1 rutabaga
- ¼ cup maple syrup
- 2 T ginger, grated (or 2 t dried)
- 1 T oil, non-coconut
- 1 t salt

Beets are a unique source of phyto-nutrients called betalains. Betanin and vulgaxanthin are the two best-studied betalains from beets, and both have been shown to provide antioxidant, anti-inflammatory, and detoxification support.

PREP TIME

Prep | 15 min
Cook | 40 min

INGREDIENTS

- 1 bag frozen collard greens (16 oz.)
- 1 T oil
- 1 onion, chopped
- 1 T Italian seasoning
- 1 t salt
- 2 tomatoes, chopped

Prep | 10 min
Cook | 15 min

ITALIAN COLLARD GREENS AND TOMATOES

DIRECTIONS

Put collards in a large pan and sauté over medium high heat until thawed and warm.

Add oil, onion, Italian seasoning, and salt. Cook for about 5 minutes.

Add chopped tomatoes and heat for 5 minutes longer, or until hot.

Tomatoes are the major dietary source of the antioxidant lycopene, which has been linked to many health benefits, including reduced risk of heart disease and cancer. They are also a great source of vitamin C, potassium, folate, and vitamin K.

MAPLE ROASTED BRUSSELS SPROUTS

INGREDIENTS

- 1½ lbs. brussels sprouts, halved
- ¼ cup oil, non-coconut
- 1 t salt
- ½ t black pepper
- 2 T maple syrup

DIRECTIONS

Preheat oven to 400° F.

In a large bowl toss all ingredients together.

Place in 9 x 13" uncovered baking dish and place in oven. Take out and stir after 10 minutes to even out the browning.

Place in oven 10 more minutes and take out and stir again. Bake for 10 more minutes for a total of 30 minutes.

Enjoy as side dish or serve over a whole grain.

Brussels sprouts contain glucosinolate, which is responsible for the bitter flavor. Cooking and digestion break down glucosinolates into compounds called isothiocyanates that have been re-searched for their anti-cancer effects, such as protecting cells from DNA damage and preventing new blood vessels from growing in tumor cells.

PREP TIME

Prep | 15 min
Cook | 30 min

MIDDLE EASTERN CHICKPEA SALAD

DIRECTIONS

In a small bowl, combine lemon juice, olive oil, garlic, and salt.

In a large bowl, combine rice, beans, tomatoes, olives, red peppers, celery, parsley, and onion and toss with lemon juice dressing.

INGREDIENTS

- ¼ cup lemon juice
- 2 T olive oil
- 1 clove garlic, crushed
- 1 t salt
- 3 ½ cups cooked brown rice
- 2 cups cooked chickpeas
- 1 pint cherry tomatoes, halved
- 1 cup pitted kalamata olives
- ¾ cup roasted red peppers, thinly sliced
- 2 stalks celery, thinly sliced
- ¼ cup fresh parsley, chopped
- ¼ cup red onion, finely diced

This recipe has all kinds of great nutrition in it. In addition to the veggies, Kalamata olives are a good source of fiber, calcium, vitamin C, vitamin A, vitamin E, and vitamin K. They also provide some mag-nesium, phosphorous and potassium as well as B vitamins.

Prep | 20 min
Cook | 5 min

BENEVOLENT
BREAKFASTS

BLUEBERRY MUFFINS

DIRECTIONS

Preheat oven to 350° F.

Mix dry ingredients, except blueberries, together well. Stir
in liquid ingredients, mix well.

Fold in blueberries last.

Pour into 12 regular size, or 24 mini muffin tins.

Bake for 20- 22 minutes.

INGREDIENTS

- 1 cup flour of choice
- 1 cup cereal or granola
- ½ cup nuts
- ¼ cup millet or sunflower seeds
- 1 T baking powder
- 1 t xanthan gum
- ½ t salt
- ½ cup soymilk
- ⅓ cup maple syrup
- ½ cup driedblueberries, or 1 cup fresh

Blueberries are a good source of Vitamin C and are high in manganese. Vitamin C is necessary for growth and development of tissues and promotes wound healing. Manganese helps the body process cholesterol and nutrients such as carbohydrates and protein.

PREP TIME

Prep | 10 min
Cook | 20 min

OVERNIGHT OATS

INGREDIENTS

- ¾ cup rolled oats
- 1 cup water
- Splash vanilla
- 2 t maple syrup
- Sprinkle of cinnamon
- Sprinkle of salt

Prep | 5 min
Cook | 0 min

DIRECTIONS

Combine all ingredients in a jar and place in the refrigerator overnight.

You can adjust the amount of water to your taste.

When ready to eat garnish with maple syrup, creamer, fresh fruit, nuts, chocolate chips, or whatever you desire.

In addition to being affordable, a variety of antioxidants known as avenanthramides are found exclusively in oats. Avenanthramides have been shown to exhibit anti-inflammatory and anti-itching activity, and may provide additional protection against coronary heart disease, colon cancer, and skin irritation. They also may play a role in controlling blood pressure.

SIMPLE HASH BROWNS

INGREDIENTS

- 2 large potatoes
- ¼ cup oil

DIRECTIONS

Grate the potatoes.

Warm oil in pan on medium low until melted.

Smash potatoes into the pan with a spatula. Cover and let it cook for 15 minutes.

Flip with a spatula and brown the other side of your potato pancake for 5 minutes.

Remove from the pan. Garnish with salt and pepper, or your favorite potato toppings.

Coconut oil contains medium chain triglycerides which may boost heart health, encourage fat burning, have antimicrobial effects, reduce hunger, reduce seizures, raise HDL (good) cholesterol, and may protect our skin, hair, and teeth.

PREP TIME

Prep | 10 min
Cook | 20 min

SPICY GRITS

INGREDIENTS

- 2 cups dry grits
- ¼ cup oil
- 1 bell pepper, finely chopped
- 2 or more jalapenos, seeded and thinly sliced
- 2 t salt
- ¼ cup nutritional yeast

Prep | 10 min
Cook | 15 min

DIRECTIONS

Cook grits according to package directions. Set aside.

In large sauté pan, sauté bell pepper and jalapenos on medium high heat in oil until peppers start to brown.

Mix in grits, salt, and nutritional yeast.

Serve hot.

Jalapeños are rich in vitamins A and C and potassium. They also have carotene an antioxidant that may help fight damage to your cells—as well as folate, vitamin K, and B vitamins. Many of their health benefits come from a compound called capsaicin.

WHOLE WHEAT WAFFLES

DIRECTIONS

Preheat the waffle maker.

In a large bowl, whisk together the dry ingredients.

Mix the wet ingredients in a smaller bowl.

Add the wet ingredients to the dry ingredients and whisk until smooth.

Spray a preheated waffle iron with non-stick cooking spray oil.

Pour about half of the batter onto the waffle iron.

Follow the waffle iron directions and cook for about 5 minutes or until the steam stops and waffle is golden brown.

Serve with margarine, powdered sugar, maple syrup, and/or fresh fruit.

Makes 2 golden waffles.

INGREDIENTS

- 1½ cups whole wheat
- pastry flour
- 1 T baking powder
- ½ t salt
- 1½ cups almond milk
- 2 T vegetable oil
- 1 t vanilla

Whole grain flours provide a good source of fiber and nutrients such as B vitamins, magnesium, and phytochemicals, including lignans and phenolic compounds. Almond milk is naturally high in vitamin E, a disease-fighting antioxidant.

PREP TIME

Prep | 10 min
Cook | 20 min

DAZZLING
DESSERTS

BANANA
BREAD
BISCUITS

INGREDIENTS

- 2 cups cashews
- ½ t salt
- 2 ripe bananas
- 1 t vanilla
- ½ cup pecans, chopped

Prep | 10 min
Cook | 20 min

DIRECTIONS

Heat oven to 350° F.

Combine cashews and salt in the food processor and process into small pieces.

Break up the bananas and add to the processor with vanilla. Mix well. Add pecans and pulse to mix.

Drop 1½ T rounds onto parchment paper or into muffin wrappers.

Bake at 350̊ for 20 minutes or until slightly firm.

Bananas contain fiber, potassium, folate, and antioxidants such as vitamin C. All of these support heart health. Bananas are also rich in the mineral potassium. Potassium helps maintain fluid levels in the body and regulates the movement of nutrients and waste products in and out of cells.

CHOCOLATE PEANUT BUTTER BARK

DIRECTIONS

In a saucepan, cook chocolate chips on low heat until melted, stirring frequently.

Add peanut butter and cook on low, stirring to combine, until melted.

Stir in vanilla.

Stir in cashews.

On a 9 x 11" parchment-lined pan, spread out chocolate mixture.

Place the pan in the refrigerator to cool and set.

Once set, cut into pieces.

As if you needed another reason to eat chocolate! The flavanols in cocoa beans, an ingredient in chocolate, are anti-oxidants, meaning that they may reduce damage to cells and lower the risk of heart disease. Some studies suggest chocolate or cocoa consumption is associated with a lower risk of insulin resistance and high blood pressure in adults.

INGREDIENTS

- Chocolate chips (10 oz.)
- 1 cup creamy peanut butter
- 1 t vanilla
- 2 cups salted cashews or almonds

PREP TIME

Prep | 5 min
Cook | 10 min

PEANUT BUTTER COOKIES

INGREDIENTS

- ½ cup flour of choice
- ½ cup oatmeal
- ½ cup natural peanut butter
- ¼ cup coconut oil, or other oil
- ¼ cup maple syrup
- 1 t xanthan gum
- ½ t vanilla extract
- ½ t salt

Prep | 10 min
Cook | 14 min

DIRECTIONS

Preheat oven to 350° F.

Mix all ingredients in bowl.

Drop rounded gooey spoonfuls onto cookie sheet.

Bake for 14-16 minutes, and let cool.

These healthy cookies contain oats for the beta-glucan fiber that is effective at reducing both total and LDL cholesterol levels. They have peanut butter for potassium, and maple syrup, the star of antioxidants.

RASPBERRY TARTS

INGREDIENTS

- 2 unfrozen ready-made
- pie crusts, or homemade pie dough
- Flour for de-sticking
- 1 jar raspberry jam

DIRECTIONS

Preheat oven to 400° F. Line baking sheet with parchment paper.

Remove pie crust from packaging. Sprinkle a little flour on your work surface and push pie crust as flat as you can get it.

Use a cookie cutter or drinking glass to make circles in the dough. Make sure to sprinkle flour under any dough that you cut so you can easily pick up the circles.

When you use up the pie crust, combine the scraps and press with fingers to make more flat dough for cutting circles.

Once you have your circles, spoon a couple of teaspoons of raspberry jam in the center.

Dip your finger in a small bowl of water and wet the circumference of the jammed circle. Place another circle on top of the jammed one and use a fork to squish together the edges to seal them.

Place tarts on parchment lined baking sheet and bake for 25 minutes.

Raspberries are high in several powerful antioxidant compounds, including vitamin C, quercetin, and ellagic acid. Raspberries are high in antioxidants, which can help reduce signs of aging by fighting free radicals in your body.

PREP TIME

Prep | 20 min

Cook | 25 min

STRAWBERRY CAKE

INGREDIENTS

DRY

- 1¾ cups whole wheat pastry flour
- 1 cup Sucanat or sugar
- 1 t baking soda
- ½ t salt

WET

- 1 cup puréed strawberries
- ½ cup vegetable oil
- 2 t vanilla extract
- 2 t apple cider vinegar

Prep | 10 min
Cook | 35 min

DIRECTIONS

Preheat oven to 350° F.

Sift flour into a large bowl.

Whisk together dry ingredients.

Whisk in wet ingredients.

Add mixture to greased bundt pan, or baking pans.

Bake for 30-35 minutes, or until inserted knife comes out clean from the center.

Allow to cool completely before frosting or glazing.

Packed with vitamins, fiber, and particularly high levels of antioxidants known as polyphenols. They are among the top 20 fruits in antioxidant capacity and are a good source of manganese and potassium.